Stop Procrastinating!

Step by Step guide to Eliminate your procrastination for good

Robert S. Clark

Table of Contents

The Four Deadly Words

Knowing Your Problem

Why Do We Procrastinate?

What's The Harm?

Excuse #1 – I'm Scared to Fail

Excuse #2 – I'm Afraid to Succeed

Excuse #3 – It's not Perfect!

Anatomy of a Non-Procrastinator

Taking the Mountains (Not the Molehills)

Write it Down!

Time Me!

Building Better Time Management

We Interrupt This Book

Rewards and Punishments

Breaking the Right Way

Get a Partner in Crime

Multitasking Will Not Help You

The Overload Trap

Don't Plan On It!

Great Scott! Look at the Time!

Head for the Hall Of Fame

The Running Back Lesson

Picture Yourself – Productive!

Make Your Fear Work For You!

The Proving Grounds

The Tortoise Was On To Something

Stop Reading and Start Today!

Inspiring Quotes

The Four Deadly Words

We've all said it. You've said it. I've said it. They're those dreaded four words that can cause so much trouble for the both of us.

"I'll do it later."

You say it when you're not in the mood to get something done. You would love to be productive, but this other thing is calling your name!

Rest assured in the fact that you're not alone. This is a classic, natural human reaction to items on our to-do list known as "procrastination."

According to The University of Warwick, people who procrastinate have a hard time starting their project, create diversions, waste time with ineffective work, rush jobs at the last minutes and often miss deadlines.

The consequences of procrastination can really bring you down, hurting your work life, your social life and multiple other aspects.

I've done it myself. I've fallen behind at work, made my loved ones angry and hurt my credit all due to putting my allotted tasks off until the very last minute. It adds unneeded stress and can really affect your health in the long run.
In this book, we will explore methods to break free from the cycle of procrastination and pain, accomplish more and live a happier, more productive life.

How do we do it? Read on, my friend, and find out!

Knowing Your Problem

It's often said the first thing you need to do in order to correct a problem in your life is owning the fact that you have a problem.

I'll start. I'm Robert Clark, and I'm a procrastinator. The irony of the fact that I'm writing a book on procrastination is not lost on me.

Dr. William Knaus of American International College co-authored *Overcoming Procrastination: Do It Now – How to Break the Procrastination Habit* and *the Procrastination Workbook: Your Personalized Program for Breaking Free of the Patterns That Hold You Back*. Procrastination, by his definition, consists of some if not all of the following symptoms:

- ➢ When faced with an unpleasant, uncomfortable task, the procrastinator substitutes a smaller, less time-pertinent, lower-priority task. Knaus dubbed these not-as-productive activities "addictivities."
- ➢ The procrastination falls into what I call The Ecclesiastes Syndrome – there's a time and a season to every purpose

under heaven – it's just that the season to accomplish what you need to isn't right now.

➢ The procrastinator needs to research the topic more.

➢ Along the same point, the procrastinator knows there's an easier way to accomplish the task they need to do. They just haven't found the way to work smarter, not harder yet. Give them a little more time.

➢ The procrastinator can't make a decision on anything, especially on something like the task ahead of them.

Does this sound like you? I know it sounds like how I am sometimes.

How do we come to this point? Check out the next chapter to find my thoughts.

Why Do We Procrastinate?

I know what I need to do when I get up in the morning. Each morning after breakfast, I write a list of things I need and want to accomplish for the day. More often than not, tasks stay on that list day after day after day.

Why does it happen? I often tell myself "Robert, you're out of time. You've done enough today. Take a break!"

The task reappears day after day, never getting crossed out, never marked complete.

Why do we procrastinate? There are multiple possibilities.

- ➢ We overestimate how much time we have left to finish our jobs.
- ➢ We overestimate our own motivation.
- ➢ We fear we will fail.

Phil Stitz and Barry Michels write the following about the reasons behind our procrastination: "We avoid every task for the same reason: Taking action will cause a certain amount of pain."

Think of something you don't want to do. Picture yourself cleaning your room, paying off those bills, finishing your homework – whatever task is hovering over your head right now.

You'll feel unpleasant, gross, repulsed by the idea of working on the task at hand. You're less than thrilled to do it.

Thinking of what we need to do, you and I both tend to retreat to our respective comfort zones. We go take a nap, surf the internet or otherwise convert our work time into leisure time.

WaitButWhy.com has a humorous way of explaining how procrastination works inside the mind. At the helm of your mind is your rational side. This side knows what it's supposed to do and makes its decisions according to what needs to be done. It looks like a tiny man at a captain's wheel.

Our little captain, however, is not alone in your mind. With him is a little monkey, representing instant gratification. While it's nice that our captain has a cute little pet to play with, Mr. IG, we'll call him, this is problematic procrastination primate.

While our captain wants to keep you going toward finishing your task, the monkey wants to head to YouTube, shop for socks, create a sculpture from saltine crackers – anything to distract you from what you're doing right now; satisfying every whim except possibly the one that matters at that moment. This monkey lives only in the here and now – forgetting what they learned in the past and neglecting how the present decisions will affect the future.

Once the monkey takes over the helm, there is one thing that can take him from the wheel – The Panic Monster. The Panic Monster manifests when a deadline is imminent and some dangerous consequence looms on the horizon.

Once the monster shows up, all hell breaks loose. When the monster takes over, you end up staying up all night to finish your work, doing a sloppier-than-planned job - just to name a few unnecessary, unwelcome consequences. Instead of earning leisure time and relaxing at the end of a rigorous work schedule, the procrastinator is in panic mode, a victim of their own cycle of unhealthy work habits and a stunted quality of life.

Delaying your assigned tasks and giving in to avoidance behaviors creates all kinds of trouble for you and those around you. Let's look at some of procrastination's poisonous side effects.

What's The Harm?

So what's the big deal if you put off until tomorrow what you can do today?

Well, my dear reader, while the tasks ahead of you may be painful, procrastination is likely much more harmful. Here are just a few of the consequences of procrastination.

Physical Consequences
- Raised blood pressure
- Stimulant dependency
- Restlessness and disruption of a healthy sleep schedule
- Tension
- Nausea

Mental/Emotional Consequences
- Lowered self-esteem
- Increased stress and worry
- Obsessive thinking
- Frustration
- Sense of helplessness

In addition to how this affects you on an individual level, think on how procrastination affects those around you.

In your work life, procrastination can bog down your career progress in both the short and the long term. If you're putting off what you need to do, you're not working effectively, and if you're not working effectively, you're not making the most of the opportunity your life affords.

Speaking of which, let's talk about how procrastination affects your overall quality of life. The task you're putting off will be blown so far out of proportion, you won't be able to see what's really important in life. Procrastination creates pessimism and with your task left undone, you'll feel as if life is passing you by.

What does procrastination do to your relationships? The procrastinator (which, in this case, is you or me) may isolate themselves, which puts unnecessary tension on the couple. You'll become less loving and giving because you're so preoccupied. On top of that, your partner may get frustrated with you and nag you to finish the task you're putting off; your partner doesn't *want* to nag you, which puts additional strain on the relationship.

In short, the point is procrastination is unhealthy for you and everyone surrounding you. When we put off until tomorrow what we can finish today, we're senselessly sacrificing a bit of our happiness both in the present and the short- and long-term futures.

With that said, what's your excuse? Maybe it's an excuse we'll debunk together further in this book. Read on.

Excuse #1 – I'm Scared to Fail

Drs. Pamela Wiegartz and Kevin Gyoerkoe analysed procrastination in a March 2011 article in *Psychology Today*. In the article, the doctors discuss three common reasons why you and I might procrastinate. The first is we're afraid to fail. Our fear of failure makes us retreat into our comfort zone; it's not unlike a turtle diving into its shell to protect itself.

While fear serves as a natural and powerful instinct to shield us from pain and other troubles, fear of failure creates anxiety, and subconsciously, we choose to avoid anything that would cause us to feel discomfort or pain, causing us to withdraw to our comfortable, unproductive shell. When you're afraid, your mind clings to hope that if you wait just long enough before the deadline hits that somehow your working conditions will improve.

When your project or task fails or isn't completed by deadline, according to *Psychology Today*, "you can rationalize that it wasn't a true test of your ability anyway – if only you had more time."

How do we beat a fear of failure? Embrace your mistakes! I'll give you example. I'm a freelance writer who once worked as a ghostwriter for a client looking for a murder mystery novel. The first week went great; a third party secured the client's payment, I got paid and he liked my work. It couldn't have worked better!

During the next two weeks, though, the project went south. The client stopped communicating and stopped paying. The third party had no payment to secure, but I made the mistake of continuing to work – for free.

Though my actions were not the reason the project failed, I made a few costly mistakes. As a result, I came away from the experience learning how to better my business and how to write a novel along the way.

My mistakes while working on the novel led to personal failure. Though I'm not at all pleased with the outcome of the project, I take the experience as valuable nonetheless. Had I procrastinated and not completed any portion of the project in a timely manner, though, I never would have come away with a valuable experience.

Yes, my dear reader, there is always a chance your project will fail or not meet the standards you're hoping to achieve. Don't let that fear hold you back! Instead, realize that whether the project or task succeeds or fails, you can always learn something form the experience. Naturally, I wish you success, but I also stress that you should confront your fears. Realize there is a chance of failure, but press on anyway!

Perhaps it's not the fear of failure that troubles you, though. Maybe it's just the opposite.

Excuse #2 – I'm Afraid to Succeed

You might ask yourself "Who's afraid of success?" Success seems like such a driving, motivating force in all aspects in our lives. We want to have a growing career, a great family, a fulfilling love life – we long to live a full life.

However, when it comes to succeeding in solving a problem or completing a project you've been putting off, with success come certain fears.

If you succeed in your efforts at work, for example, perhaps your boss will see this and give you additional responsibilities (and additional pay). When you're given more responsibilities, your co-workers might see you as more of a reader and look to you for help and leadership.

It takes hard work to succeed (meet one of your goals) and it takes harder work to be successful (take yourself to the next level in some aspect of your life). Like those who use their fear of failure as a reason to procrastinate, those who fear conquering their procrastination will lead to success seek to remain in their comfort zones.

When you succeed in any aspect of your life, you'll face self-actualization, or, to quote the U.S. Army, being all you can be. By avoiding and putting off the tasks and challenges ahead of you, yes, you'll stay in your comfort zone, but you miss out on knowing the limits of what you can really do with your life.

Don't run away from opportunities for success! Run *to* them! Just be careful not to fall into the next type of excuse.

Excuse #3 – It's not Perfect!

I admit that sometimes I can be a bit of a perfectionist. I'm a former newspaper editor, and I was in charge of, among other responsibilities, designing the newspaper.

I wanted to make sure everything looked just right; with the clock ticking toward deadline, I struggled to make sure every word, every photo, every advertisement was to-the-pixel precisely where it needed to be.

This need for perfection, combined with my tendency to procrastinate, sometimes made me quite late for deadline, which made my work life suffer.

"Perfectionism may underlie your avoidance," said Weigartz and Gyoerkoe in *Psychology Today*. "Because you believe that things should be done perfectly, the result is that nothing gets done at all. When faced with a task, you become overwhelmed and frustrated – paralyzed by impossible standards."

I struggle to think of an everyday problem so large that working on fixing it rather than putting it off for another day won't bring about a solution.

The problem or task ahead of you isn't going anywhere, and you aren't going anywhere without fixing the problem or completing the task.

What if it's not perfect? Work through the issues. Decide what's ultimately important and what can be overlooked. For example, I got married in 2013, and I remember helping my then-fiancée plan the wedding. We had so much we wanted to prepare for the guests, and most of it went off without a hitch. There were a few items on our checklist that remained unchecked, but I got to the wedding on time, our rings weren't lost and all the people who said they were coming came to the wedding. The core of the wedding and the events that surrounded it was solid; everything else was icing on the cake.

When it comes to wrestling with perfectionism and procrastination, make a list of your priorities, starting with the most important. Give yourself a deadline (if you don't already have one) and diligently, every day, work your way down the list. Once the deadline is upon you, you should have your basic needs met and maybe a few bonuses added on to it.

You don't have to be perfect. Your project or task doesn't have to be perfect. To quote the first boss I ever had, by the end of the day, your work should be "perfect enough."

In the case of any of these fears and you find yourself getting antsy and nervous, take a deep breath. Inhale for five heartbeats, hold your breath and exhale for five heartbeats. Your pulse will slow down and you should feel your body relax a bit. Once the feeling has passed, carry on.

Procrastination can certainly take its toll on your self esteem, making you feel like you're not "enough." What do non-procrastinators have that you don't? Perhaps the next chapter will shed some light on what makes a person a non-procrastinator.

Anatomy of a Non-Procrastinator

As a point of pre-emptive clarification, a "non-procrastinator" is *not* someone who does not procrastinate at all. In fact, according to psychology expert Kendra Cherry, procrastination itself is a human tendency and isn't necessarily an indication of a big problem.

However, if you're like me and you're reading this book, procrastination, for people like you and I, is a chronic problem. The problem is deeper than having poor time management skills.

"Non-procrastinators focus on the task that needs to be done," said psychologist Dr. Joseph Ferrari. "They have a stronger personal identity and are less concerned about what psychologists call 'social esteem.'" Ferrari defines social esteem as a concern for how others perceive us.

What does this mean? Think of it this way. Our friend Joe is hard at work on his project. Terry and Jerry don't care for Joe's hard-working nature because it makes them look bad; they might see him as a threat to their livelihood (to some degree) and may dislike Joe as a result.

Joe, being a self-disciplined worker who seldom procrastinates, disregards Terry's and Jerry's attitudes toward him and continues on with the task.

Those who don't procrastinate are conscientious, self-disciplined in many aspects of their lives, persistent and more personally responsible.

Fictitious though he may be, Joe's attitude is an example for you and I – his hard work and discipline in avoiding procrastination will surely be rewarded.

How do we become more motivated and self-disciplined, though? How do we become non-procrastinators?

I have good news, my dear reader. For as many ways as there are to procrastinate and distract yourself from the task at hand, there are just as many to keep yourself focused, on-task and working hard! Read on.

Taking the Mountains (Not the Molehills)

I'm nearly 30 years old, and I love video games. I've been playing video games since the days of the NES. I got my first system when I was 6 years old and I was hooked.

I still play every now and again these days, but I have my own responsibilities to handle first. When it comes to video and computer games, I occasionally liked to challenge myself by setting the game on the highest difficulty just to see what would happen.

I never did that great, but it was still fun to try!

In the case of conquering procrastination, you'd really benefit from "playing on hard mode," or taking down your most unsavory, uncomfortable tasks first.

Why is that? When you get up in the morning, after you've had your morning coffee or tea and breakfast, your energy level is high. Your big task, the one you really want to put off but in the back of your mind you *know* you shouldn't, is the one you should tackle first while your strength for the day is at its highest. If you move around your mountain and start stamping out the molehills, you're going to wear yourself out and not be able to finish what really matters at the end of the day – that nasty, gross project that's still there and so easily could have been squashed and put away.

Even if the tasks you complete rather than your "mountain," there are two problems: 1. The mountain's still there, unchipped. and 2. You're not really present when it comes to handling the molehills because the mountain still looms over you. In short, you're not doing as good of a job as you could be if you would have first handled the most unpleasant task in the first place.

Here's how to fix it. Think about everything you need to do for the day. Identify the task that leaves the worst taste in your mouth; the one you find the most unpleasant or uncomfortable. Finish it first.

On the same note, it might help you to understand why you don't want to finish a particular task. Always question why you choose not to complete a particular task. Why don't you want to finish that business report? Why don't you want to finish building the deck? Why don't you want to give your mother a call?

Once you dig deep and understand why you don't want to do these things, the task itself may not look as bad without a big, legitimate and timely reason to back it up.

If you take some time to think of why the "mountain" is more important than the molehills you've been stamping, think about what the worst thing is about not finishing the most unpleasant task. Even if it's a small reason like you'll be annoyed with yourself for a short period of time, keep in mind the small actions and thoughts – for the better or for worse – can and do have bigger consequences in the future.

If you get the bad jobs done first, you can focus more on the jobs you should do as well as the jobs you *want* to do.

In the next chapter, we'll look more into how to better organize yourself and what you need to do for the day!

Write it Down!

When I was a kid and occasionally forgot or put off items I needed to do, she would tell me again and again "Write it down!"

Mom would smile to know that her advice is going in a book now. To make an effective to-do list, you should write down everything you have to do for the day or week – whichever works better for you. Break activities into smaller bits if you feel that's necessary. Cross off each item as you work through them; as your list starts to shrink, your pride in your productivity and a job well done will grow!

When you choose to break bigger tasks into smaller tasks, don't stress yourself out! You don't need to know every small step right now; the first few will suffice. If you continue to plan well, everything will fall into place!

Here are a few tips to build an effective to-do list:

➢ Focus on the items you would normally put off rather than the ones you know you would complete regularly.

Try dividing the list into three different categories: what needs to be done, what probably should be done and what you want to do – in that order.

➢ Consider setting timed deadlines for yourself. Rather than "Call Mom," write "Call Mom by 2:00."

➢ When you get a moment during the course of the day (and not too long of a moment – you don't want to fall back into procrastination, after all!), check your list again and figure out what items are of high priority. Complete the highest priority items first.

➢ Keep a journal throughout the day. When something comes to mind that requires your attention in the near future, write it down. You will need to include these items in tomorrow's to-do list. Focus on today's to-do list for now.

➢ When it comes to bi, high priority projects, break it down into steps to accomplish each day. Your future self will thank you!

➢ When you come across an item on your to-do list that you really don't want to deal with right now and you're tempted to procrastinate – **STOP!** Before you think of uttering those four deadly words, consider the two-minute rule. Ask yourself "Will this take me less than two minutes to finish?" If the answer is yes, do it and get it out of the way. Force yourself to use those two minutes to be productive rather than push off the little tasks that will just cause you trouble later.

The to-do list can be a very effective tool when it comes to tackling the procrastination problem. But what if I told you you might be able to conquer procrastination just by checking your watch? Read on to find out how!

Time Me!

When I was a kid, my siblings and I used to race each other up and down our driveway. Back then, I won more often than not, being the oldest and the tallest. If we tried that now, though, I'm not so sure I'd come out on top.

What's the point to my little story? A time limit is a compelling tool we use in our everyday lives to motivate ourselves to accomplish even the most unpleasant tasks.

You might not even realize it's happening, but when you think about it, timed events are all around us! You have to be at work at a certain time or you could get in trouble, possibly losing your livelihood. You need to turn in your school assignment on time or you will be penalized.

As we touched on briefly in the last chapter, using timed deadlines can help you develop self-discipline and help you overcome your procrastination problem.

Here's what you need to do:

- ➤ Set a time period in which you do nothing but work. Start with 10 minutes.
- ➤ Remove all sources of distraction. Get away from your TV, your cell phone, books, magazines, your refrigerator – anything that will derail you from the task at hand.
- ➤ Force yourself to do nothing but the job at hand for 10 minutes before going back to your distraction.
- ➤ Following the 10-minute work period, you might find that you'll end up in a mental "groove;" you've started a job and now that you've gained some momentum, you don't want to stop! When you keep working at a fast but careful pace to accomplish as much as you can in that 10-minute period of time, you're developing self-discipline.

Using the same principal of working in timed bursts, one tried-and-true method of conquering procrastination is to time-box your tasks. For each item on your to-do list, assign a specific amount of time to finish the task. If you don't finish your task in the allotted amount of time, move on to the next task. When you reach the bottom of the list, start again from the top with the same amount of time.

This trains your brain into believing you can't afford to waste time, so you must take action.

If the timed approach sounds like something that might work for you, perhaps you can combine it with the practices listed in the next section – creating a time management kit!

Building Better Time Management

When it comes to working on any job, you're only as good as your tools. Conquering your procrastination habit once and for all is no different! Try equipping yourself with some or all of About.com Expert Grace Fleming's toolbox, listed below, to maximize your productivity at home or at work!

1. **Web Page Timer** – When we log on to social media websites or play games online, it's often difficult to understand how much time you spend browsing or gaming. Fortunately, a number of tools have emerged to help internet users track their activity. For example, StayFocused on Google Chrome helps track the time you spend on your online guilty pleasures and time wasters. The free application allows you to pick the pages that are your "worst offenders" and track how much time you waste. Keeping yourself accountable is key!

2. **Work Timer** – On the other side of the coin, sometimes you'll find yourself working too long on a particular project. Keep a stopwatch (there are some available online) or a timer nearby and track each task you work on. Look for ways to make yourself more efficient. This

will free up more time for both leisure and tackling those long-put-off tasks!

3. **To Do List** – A few chapters ago, we discussed how to build an effective to-do list. There's nearly nothing quite as critical to your success as a good to-do list. Carry a notepad with you at all times and when a potential to-do item crosses your mind or is told to you, write it down immediately (Listen to me; I'm channeling my mother!)! As you finish each task, project and step, cross them off to keep track of where you are. If there are not enough hours in a day to get your list all done, carry over items to the next day. Make sure, however, you don't leave those items on for too long!

4. **Wall Calendar** – In your workspace, keep a big wall calendar. Write down different due dates and deadlines using either post-it notes stuck on critical dates or a bright-colored pen or marker. That way, whenever you come into your workspace, you'll notice the calendar and the approaching deadlines, serving as a constant reminder of what needs to be done.

5. **Sticky Note Flags** – On a similar note, little sticky note flags listing the tasks you need to placed in strategic locations around the house to remind you of what needs

to be done! Try sticking these notes on door knobs, around the bathroom mirror, on your bed post, dresser – wherever you need to!

6. **Cell Phone Calendar** – Nearly every cell phone nowadays carries some sort of calendar program. As using a cell phone alarm clock can be an effective tool for waking you up or letting you know when dinner is ready, you can also use the calendar to remind you of when projects are due. Try setting an alarm the day or even a few hours before a particular project is due to make sure you have everything done as best as it can be.

7. **Bedside Notebook** – You've been there. So have I. An idea or a reminder pops into your head in the middle of the night. You sit bolt upright and try to hold on to that thought until morning. When morning comes around, the thought is gone! Hold on to that thought by writing it down in your notebook. You can also use this to create another to-do list before settling into bed.

8. **Sleep Aids** – Getting those eight hours a day may not be what you need. Sometimes better sleep in any given amount of time (be it a nap or all overnight) can really prevent you from beating up your snooze button. If you

fall asleep with a sleep mask or some soothing white noise to get to sleep.

9. **Waking Aids** – On the other hand, if you have a hard time getting out of bed in the morning, maybe you need a new, more effective alarm clock. You can set two alarms for yourself or find a clock that vibrates your bed or flashes lights. When browsing online one day, I found an alarm clock that rings and actively runs away from you while ringing! Maybe that's the clock we both need!

Give a few (or all) of these tools a try to create a more productive you!

Speaking of being more productive, do you ever catch yourself being your own interruption? If you're like me, you do! Read on to see how to fix it.

We Interrupt This Book

If you're like me, my mind *wants* to be productive, really; there are just so many good and interesting things out in the world that need our attention first.

Like you, I start off on the right track. I work on what I need to work on and then suddenly, my train of thought hits a junction and veers off in another direction altogether.

It goes something like this:

"Well, it's time to get some writing done. It's looking good so far."

"Wait, she posted *what* on Facebook?"

"Hang on a second, Robert, come back, come back. You have a book to write."

"But look how awesome this YouTube video is! Oh, the laundry's done!"

"No, we can't stop writing, or..."

"What we really need is a snack!"

My mind, some days, does not naturally embrace what it needs to do. Most of the time, it's the very technology I use to build my independent business that becomes the downfall of what my productivity could be.

However, there's technology available to help curb unproductive uses of your time and harness the technology for your work!

➢ Freedom – (macfreedom.com, $10) kills the Internet connection for a certain period of time. Sure, you can reconnect to the internet – if you want to go to the hassle of rebooting your computer!

➢ RescueTime (rescuetime.com, free) looks at every move you make online and shows them back to you in easy-to-read charts. The results will either disgust you or fill you with glee, depending on how you used your time. It's truly an impartial way to track the time you spend online!

➢ LeechBlock (addons.mozilla.org, free) is a Firefox add-on that blocks certain sites during a designated work time. For example, if you're tempted to check your Facebook page during your work hours, LeechBlock puts the page out of reach.

Whatever it is that interrupts your workflow, take measures to remove it from your view or reach if you don't trust yourself to have the potential distractions in the same room with you.

Instead, you might consider using these distractions as prizes of sorts honoring your productivity. Find out how you can achieve more through the use of punishment and rewards in the next chapter!

Rewards and Punishments

For decades – dare I say centuries – psychiatrists and therapists (even parents) have employed reinforcement and punishment to change and enforce behavior patterns. In a nutshell, reinforcement is when you do something well and are rewarded as a consequence. Punishment is a penalty for bad behavior.

You can use this basic principal of psychology to help conquer procrastination once and for all!

- **Positive Reinforcement:** If you complete your to-do list, reward yourself! Pick a reward that motivates you – go out to eat, see a movie, hang out with your friends!
- **Negative Reinforcement:** Let's say you complete your to-do list on a Friday night. You can reward yourself by taking an item or two off your to-do list. If you finish cleaning out the garage, for example, you don't have to run out for errands during the weekend. Take away something you don't want to do when you complete a major project.
- **Punishment:** Don't allow yourself certain niceties unless you finish an allotted task. Don't take a nap, chat

with your friends, play video games or what have you until the task is done. Once it's complete, you can reward yourself.

If your procrastination is particularly severe, consider this punishment. Give someone you trust $50 and tell them to keep it if you don't complete a certain project in an allotted period of time. Money is a powerful motivational tool!

As with all things, timing is key. How can you use your breaks and rewards most effectively? Read on to find out!

Breaking the Right Way

Taking a break seems like the last thing that should be discussed in a book about procrastination. However, procrastination is break time abused. In this chapter, we'll touch on how to break the right way!

The whole point of taking a break is to avoid burning out. To make the most of your break, be sure to get up and walk around – don't just stay at the desk! After about an hour or 90 minutes of working, stand up and go for a short walk, grab a snack, go get some water – whatever you need in order to just decompress and recharge for a moment.

If your self-enforced punishments and reinforcements don't work, you can always work with someone!

Along the same lines, some people work better after a short coffee break, others while listening to music or even with silence. Everyone is different and each has a different "zone." The key to maximizing your productivity is understanding what helps you be the most productive. However, you should be careful when creating your own work environment and rhythm. You don't want to create conditions that are too relaxed; if you fall into too leisurely of an environment, you might be inadvertently encouraged to fall into procrastination again! Once you fall into a good, balanced zone, though, you'll want to take on your most difficult or hated tasks first while your mood and energy are at their highest.

Whatever you decide to do as far as creating a work environment that maximizes your productivity, make sure it's clean. If your house or desk or workspace is cluttered, clean it up. Throw away the trash and do away with things you don't need right then. This will make for a much less stressful and more positive working environment.

You can do a lot to help yourself, but don't be too proud to ask for help! Find out how a friend or loved one can help you really kick the habit!

Get a Partner in Crime

When you have a problem you feel you might not be able to handle on your own. If there's one thing I've learned in my life, it's to not be too proud to ask for help.

Perhaps a friend or a family member can help by holding you accountable. This doesn't have to be anything formal. Simply tell your friend or loved one about the project you're working on.

Telling your friend or loved one about your big project will motivate you. How? If you're progressing nicely on your project, tell your friend or loved one about teach step. Their pride in you will bolster you to want to continue doing a good job. On the other side of the coin, if you don't accomplish as much as you would like to, you'll endure the embarrassment of admitting a setback or failure. Nobody wants that.

While it's great to work as hard as you can and have a friend help you along, it's also important to work as *smart* as you can. For more on that, turn to the next page.

Multitasking Will Not Help You

There are probably a lot of people you know who pride themselves on their ability to handle multiple tasks at a time. It's certainly a skill that has its place and purpose and they should rightly take pride in what they do.

However, when it comes to procrastination, multitasking is not going to help you complete the top item on your to-do list effectively.

Multitasking, on its face, appears to accomplish more in less time; after all, you're tackling multiple projects at once! What could possibly be wrong with that?

By multitasking, you're dividing your attention between multiple tasks; if any of the given tasks aren't getting your full attention, you won't complete any of them in a high-quality manner. If you multitask too much, you may find yourself having to re-do several of the tasks you accomplished by multitasking because they weren't don the first time around. This lengthens your to-do list, the opposite of your ultimate goal!

Complete the first task, *and then* move on to the next. A long to-do list is a big temptation to multitask, but you must resist. Quality will always outweigh quantity when it comes to day-to-day tasks. Invest wisely in your priority tasks; your future self will thank you!

Procrastination and ineffective multitasking can take a serious toll on your mind and body. In the next chapter, we'll dive deeper into the mental toll procrastination and multi-tasking can have on your mind.

The Overload Trap

The night before I got married, I was worried.

Was I going to be a good husband? What would happen if I wasn't ready for everything? Would I remember what to do come the wedding ceremony?

My brothers-in-law invited me out for dinner as a "bachelor party" of sorts and I made my worries known to them; that I had been turning the marriage over and over again inside my head – thoughts buzzing around like so many angry bees.

My brother-in-law offered three words of advice that I took to heart – "Don't overthink it."

With any undertaking of any kind, a little thinking and planning can go a long way. However, I advise you not to spend too much time on it. You can't plan for every possibility, and I know you and I both want to try, but the fact of the matter is we simply can't do it.

When it comes to your project, it's vital to *work* on the actual project, not just to *plan* it. As humans, we can't plan perfectly. The key is to plan the steps of what you need to do to complete the task, and leave it at that. Put the pen down and get to work. If something should go wrong or the conditions change, you can and you will adapt. Don't worry. Take action!

There's a second purpose to writing down a basic, step-by-step plan. Taking on a large project is like eating a turkey – eating the entire thing in one piece is overwhelming and seems quite impossible (and silly). However, cutting the turkey – and the task – into pieces that are more physically manageable pieces makes the task seen much simpler.

Come up with a plan and take action one step at a time. No matter the project, you can do it if you focus on one step at a time.

When it comes to planning, there's a very basic, often overlooked tip to avoid procrastination.

Don't Plan On It!

That's right.

There are many ways to avoid procrastination, but perhaps one of the simplest is to not plan on procrastinating.

How do you do it? If you've wrestled with procrastination, chances are this dialogue has gone through your head before:

"I wonder if I have time to clean my room today…"

"No, no, I can't do that on Thursday night. I'm going to be up all night writing a paper instead."

If you find yourself aboard this train of thought, stop for a moment and think about what you're saying to yourself. With that mindset, you're *planning* to procrastinate! You may be enabling your problem without ever realizing it!

On the bright side, this kind of thinking shows you have the planning skills you need to get out of your predicament. The key to conquering procrastination in this way is to be aware of when you're planning to procrastinate and plan far enough ahead and get a little work done each day so you don't have to plan to procrastinate. You have the tools you need in your head – it's a matter of using them in the right way!

Speaking of planning ahead, perhaps to conquer procrastination, you need to travel to the future…

Great Scott! Look at the Time!

I am not a morning person. I used to dread having to wake up at the wee hours of the morning to open the restaurant where I used to work. I didn't want to prepare food and coffee. I didn't want to interact with my co-workers, to say nothing of the early-rising customers. Aside from a paycheck, getting up that early in the morning to get things done was not something I wanted to do.

When it comes to procrastination, I feel like you and I have a "not a morning person" mentality all the time. We don't want to get started on work. It's still early. There's plenty of time for that later, right?

Be careful when you find yourself coming across that thought in your head! Before you fall into the "morning person" trap, try giving yourself a new primary deadline.

What do I mean by that? Let's ay you have a paper due on the 15th of this coming month. Give yourself a new deadline – have it done by the 12th instead!

You may have to make a concentrated effort to force yourself to stick to your new primary deadline, but trust that the extra effort is worth it. By adhering to a new deadline, you leave yourselves with a few drama-free days to move on to the next steps on your to-do list.

An added benefit of moving your deadline up by a day or three is the avoidance of Murphy's Law. Murphy's Law dictates that "Whatever can go wrong, *will* go wrong." If you trim your own personal deadline down in such a way that it's a few days ahead of the actual deadline, you have extra time in which to correct any mistakes or "monkey wrenches" that are thrown into an otherwise on-track project. If you end up not needing the extra time you've allowed yourself, you come home with a sense of accomplishment and a job well done – and ahead of time, no less!

Besides feeling you work better under pressure, another common excuse for procrastination is a lack of inspiration. If you're like me, perhaps getting is sometimes not enough "inspiration" to get the job done. However, there are inspiring people all around you, if you know where to look…

Head for the Hall Of Fame

We all have heroes in our lives. My wife comes readily to mind for me; she's inspired so much positive change in my life and I admire her attitude regarding her work and her faith, among many other things.

I feel I'm a better man today than I was a year ago because of her. She's influenced me and my life and I can only hope I've done the same for her.

The point is when you're working to break away from procrastination, who you spend your time with really matters. In the case of breaking your habit, spend some time with people who motivate you.

Everyone knows a leader – someone people look up to, someone people see as a man or woman of action. Spend more time with your hall-of-famers; people you want to emulate, in this case, people who go forth and get things done.

In our modern world, we're certainly not short of venues of communication. Call them. Text them. Message them on social networking.

If you know someone who has accomplished a big project identical or very similar to yours, all the better for you! Find them, communicate with them and discuss the project and goals with them. Realize the goal you're working toward is possible and your friend or colleague is proof!

Touching on what we discussed earlier, have your hall-of-famer keep you accountable and spur you on to finish your project faster than you may have had you worked completely alone.

Misery isn't the only thing that loves company – motivation isn't a solo act either.

Knowing there are people who have gone before you and accomplished what you seek to accomplish is a powerful motivational tool. In our next chapter, we'll look at a case study a psychologist learned in his school days.

The Running Back Lesson

The authors we cite within this book have stories of their own to share of people they look up to. That's right – the very people who I learned from learned from so many people themselves how to be all they could be.

In the case of Greatist author Phil Stutz, he learned an important lesson on motivation from an unlikely source.

When he was in high school, Phil befriended a football star – a running back – when they bonded of a shared ineptitude of drawing.

When they started talking, the football player explained why he was one of the city's finest running backs. While the player wasn't the fastest, most agile or cleverest of running backs, the thing that made him special was he was not afraid of being tackled.

He embraced being tackled, so to speak. Phil wasn't a big guy as a teenager; he was about half the size of the football player!

He couldn't understand why the football player wanted to be tackled, but the player went on to explain his logic.

Most running backs tend to try to avoid tacklers in order to progress down the field. Phil's friendly football player took a more maverick approach, instead picking a defensive target and charge at them. He knew what he was getting himself into. He didn't avoid the pain. He welcomed it.

The point is when this football player charged at his pain, the pain wouldn't have as much power over him. He turned his pain into power; he faced the pain before him and moved through it.

Whatever project you're facing, you can face it head-on knowing that the pain and unpleasantness you're going through won't last forever. In the next chapter, we'll discuss how to use your mind to conquer your matters!

Picture Yourself – Productive!

Visualization and imaginations can be powerful tools – it can work for you or against you.

On one side of the coin, imagination can fuel your fears. What happens if you fail? What could go wrong? Everything could go wrong?! Remember – fear leads to excuses, excuses lead to procrastination, and procrastination leads to all sorts of awful, avoidable outcomes.

On the other hand, though, visualization can spur you on when you're feeling down, lazy or like straying toward procrastination.

Look to the future, long after the task is done. Picture yourself doing your favorite leisure time activity, free of the burden of the task you're taking on right now. Think of how proud your loved ones and colleagues will be when the job is done.

You have the power to make that future happen so long as you keep on trucking! You can do it!

Your imagination and visualization skills aren't the only mental functions you can harness in increase your procrastination prevention power!

Make Your Fear Work For You!

As we'd mentioned in our previous chapters, fear is a powerful feeling at the very core of our being. It's natural to be afraid.

We've gone through a couple of ways in which fear can lead excuses, which leads to procrastination. However, making your fear work for you can get you back on track.

Rather than focusing on the fear that leads to you excusing yourself from the task at hand, I want you to go to your desk and take up a pen and piece of paper. Instead of writing why you're afraid to get started or continue on your project, write down what will happen in the long run if you *don't* act now!

If you don't work, nothing gets done. If nothing gets done, nothing changes. If there's no productivity, there's no progress, and if people depend on you for progress, you could find yourself in a heap of trouble.

Visualization and working on your mindset are all well and good, but it's also important to take it that one, critical step further – Prove your procrastination prevention practices to yourself!

The Proving Grounds

Conquering procrastination is a tough thing for any of us to do; you're not alone by any means! I, for one, am in the same boat you are.

Getting in the right mindset and applying practices go hand hint hand when you want to squash your procrastination habits once and for all. In the end, the one person to whom you have to prove your procrastination-pulverizing abilities is yourself. Here's how to do it.

Aside from basic life functions, nearly everything you and I do, say and think on a daily basis is a choice. Maybe you can take some time throughout the day to write down some of the choices you made; a "done" list if you will.

Let me give you a prime example. Right now, I could have chosen to do a number of things around the house – clean the bathroom, catch up on the newest premieres of my favorite TV shows, take up knitting – anything. Instead of making choices that don't adhere to my to-do list, I've chosen to write this book for your benefit and for my own as well. You don't have to go to work – but it's probably a good idea. You're not forced to work; you can choose not to, but you didn't, so even something as simple as that can go on the done list.

To be as productive as you can at the right time, you'll need to suppress your urge to satisfy the part of your mind that looks for instant gratification. Maybe some of these tips will help!

- Make your tasks real. This ties in to another point I made earlier; tell your friends and family about the tasks you have on your to-do list and have them hold you accountable.
- Set an event. What do I mean? Let's say you want to build a deck onto your home. Let's say there's about six months of work to be done (having the home improvement skills of a dull crayon, I don't know if this is accurate or not when starting from scratch). Seven months from today, schedule an event on Facebook if you have it (or send out snail-mail or e-mail invitations) to a big barbecue as a "deck warming" party. This gives you a firm deadline and as an extra bonus, your hungry guests will keep you accountable!
- Leave post-it notes around the house, along with your regular to-do reminders, listing some of the good choices

you made in the past few days. You'll thank your past self and gain that little morale boost it might take to get going on those pesky tasks.

- If you're trying to learn a new hobby or skill for your work, business or other important aspect of your life (yes, even leisure is important!), make a non-refundable investment. If you want to get in shape, for example, pay for a year's membership at the gym. Better get moving! You don't want that money to go to waste, do you?

If some of these motivational tools aren't working for you, do a checkup. Throw out the methods that don't work for you and concentrate on those that do.

In all of this work to conquer your procrastination habit, it's very important to realize that you realize this is a slow and steady process. In the next chapter, we'll talk about how you can prepare yourself for the road ahead.

The Tortoise Was On To Something

I think it's safe to say that you and I are familiar with the tale of the Tortoise and the Hare. One of Aesop's most famous fables, the quick-footed, arrogant Hare challenges the slow Tortoise to a race. The Hare was so confident in his abilities, he gave the Tortoise a head start. The Hare dawdled throughout the race, but the Tortoise just kept right on trucking, doggedly pursuing his goal.

The Tortoise eventually wins. Most interpretations of what Aesop was trying to say was dogged determination and persistence no matter the speed and obstacles will be rewarded in the end.

Think of beating procrastination as your "race." This is your obstacle. This is my obstacle, too. Step by step, brick by brick, practice and build yourself up to break away from procrastination. There's no shortcut when it comes to changing the way you think or the way you behave, even if you wouldn't characterize yourself as a particularly stubborn person.

For example, I'm a classic overthinker and very much my own worst enemy, especially when it comes to procrastination. I've felt a loss of self-respect, self-esteem, confidence among many other things. Don't let yourself fall into that trap! Instead, tell yourself to get up, dust yourself off and try again. The past is what it is, but you're not there anymore. You're in the present and there are new, better opportunities before you.

You're not aiming for perfection – remember, we talked about the dangers of perfectionism earlier in this book. You should really be aiming for improvement. Think of it as investing in your future. If you were to take $20 from one paycheck and deposit them into a bank account you leave untouched, you'll be $20 richer next week. In this day and age $20 really isn't going to get you very much at all. However, if you keep this habit going for 20 years, you'll have a nice little fund tucked away for emergencies, a well-earned vacation or who knows what else!

When you change your habits for the better, you're investing in a better future for yourself. If you take it upon yourself to improve and move away from your procrastination problem this week, you'll be a little better off next week. In a year, you'll be a much more productive, changed-for-the-better person!

As with the larger items on your to-do list, break your procrastination prevention progress into little, digestible pieces. You're not moving from Point A to Point Z right away. Start with B and move on from there. Instead of committing to a complete transformation of yourself like a phoenix rising from so many ashes, change one thing at a time. If you're trying to lose weight, commit to working out once this week. If you have a home improvement project to complete, set aside one or two hours a day to work on your project. Keep to those smaller commitments, and you'll start to notice a trend. You'll gain momentum when it comes to taking on your projects, completing them and moving on to even more.

Stop Reading and Start Today!

I hope this journey through procrastination prevention practices has been as educational for you as it has for me.

After all that's been said, it's time for you and I to part ways, go forth and take the most important step – Start!

Once you start building momentum, you'll hone your work habits to make yourself more productive, working smarter rather than harder. It takes a few weeks and a great deal of practice and discipline to develop good habits, but I have absolute faith in you.

To start developing a good work track record, commit to coming out of your shell and comfort zone and force yourself to work on something you've been putting off at least once a day.

Set aside your excuses. Squash your fear. Face your laziness and push past it. Don't forget to reward yourself for a job well done!

You don't have to take on a huge project right off the bat. Start small and work your way up. Keep moving forward.

Tim Urban of WaitButWhy.com succinctly sums up why you should always work on the big projects of life. So much rides on procrastination. There's a reason "follow your dreams" is such a huge phrase – so much so, it's become a cliché. In order to be happy with the way you live your life, you really should work toward your goals every day. The task might not be particularly pleasant for the present, but your future will be all the richer for the effort you put into the tasks before you. Your self-esteem, the regrets that burden you, your relationships, the fulfillment you get out of life – it can all be improved by doing today what you *could* put off until tomorrow – *but won't.*

Take action, and you will reap the rewards! Your future self will thank you.

Inspiring Quotes

"Tomorrow is often the busiest day of the week."
Spanish Proverb

"If you want to make an easy job seem mighty hard, just keep putting off doing it."
Olin Miller

"Putting off an easy thing makes it hard. Putting off a hard thing makes it impossible."
George Claude Lorimer

"In a moment of decision, the best thing you can do is the right thing to do, the next best thing is the wrong thing, and the worst thing you can do is nothing."
Theodore Roosevelt

"Nothing is so fatiguing as the eternal hanging on of an uncompleted task"
William James